THE LONDON BOROUGH

C000116911

ORI

Please return this item by the last date stamped below, to the library from which it was borrowed.

Renewals
Any item may be renewed twice by telephone or post, provided it is not required by another customer. Please quote the barcode number.

Overdue Charges
Please see library notices for the current rate of charges levied on overdue items. Please note that the overdue charges are made on junior books borrowed on adult tickets.

A £19.99

Postage
Postage on overdue notices is payable.   RESERVE STOCK

94 - 2707073		
due 10/04/06		
		92.0

"All of Christ's faithful,
whatever be the conditions, duties,
and circumstances of their lives,
will grow in holiness day by day
through these very situations..."

Vatican II: Constitution on the Church, 41

FELICITY O'BRIEN

THE
CHEERFUL GIVER

Margaret Sinclair

 St Paul Publications

Acknowledgements: The passages quoted in this book are taken from: D.E. Burton, *Margaret Sinclair*, The Margaret Sinclair Centre; F.A. Forbes, *Margaret Sinclair*, Sands, London 1940 (4th ed.), and from the "Positio". Quotations from *Lumen Gentium*, CTS, London 1965. The Scripture quotations herein are from Revised Standard Version of the Bible, Catholic edition, copyright 1965 and 1966 by the division of the Christian Education of the National Council of the Churches of Christ in the USA, and are used by permission. All rights reserved.

St Paul Publications
Middlegreen, Slough SL3 6BT, England

Copyright © St Paul Publications 1989
Printed by the Society of St Paul, Slough
Cover by Mary Lou Winters, FSP
ISBN 0 85439 310 2

St Paul Publications is an activity of the priests and brothers of the Society of St Paul who promote the Gospel through the media of social communication

Contents

Preface

It gives me great pleasure to introduce this short book dealing with the life of the Venerable Margaret Sinclair in the new series *Images of Holiness*.

About two years ago I was asked to take on the work of promoting the cause for the beatification and canonization of the Venerable Margaret Sinclair, also known as Sister Mary Francis of the Five Wounds. Although I have spent many years of my priestly life in Edinburgh, the city where she was born, I have to confess that I knew little about her life. Since my appointment as Vice-Postulator for her cause I have become aware of the need for more literature. Most of the pamphlets published over the years are now out of print and yet the interest in the life of Margaret Sinclair appears to be on the increase.

This interest is not confined to Edinburgh or indeed Scotland. I receive letters from as far afield as Canada, the United States, Australia, New Zealand and many other places throughout the world. These letters are requests for prayer leaflets and almost invariably literature. This little book is, therefore, most welcome.

Margaret Sinclair was born 29th March

1900. She was baptized a fortnight after birth at St Patrick's Church, just off the High Street on the south side of Edinburgh which is the historic heart of the city. She attended school at St Anne's and was taught by the Sisters of Mercy. At 14 years of age she left school to begin work as an apprentice French- polisher. A few years later she became friendly with a young man and was engaged to be married. The engagement was broken off and at this point she went on retreat with her sister Bella (happily still with us and living in the Convent of the Little Sisters of the Poor here in Edinburgh).

It was already recognized by her contemporaries that she was a holy person, something special. However, her spiritual life deepened and she began to think seriously about the religious life. She had heard that the Poor Clares Convent at Liberton in Edinburgh was in need of help. The seed was planted and she applied to Liberton Convent for acceptance. She wished to be an extern Poor Clare sister but there was no vacancy and so she was referred to the Poor Clares at Notting Hill in London. She entered the convent at Notting Hill 22nd July 1923. She was clothed as novice 11th February 1924 and made her first profession of vows 14th February, 1925. Within a few months she became ill. Tuberculosis was diagnosed and she was moved to a sanatorium at Warley in Essex. Her condition worsened and the illness ended in death 24th November 1925. Her body was returned to the convent and she was buried at Kensal Green Cemetery, London. On 21st December 1927 her body was transferred to Mount Vernon Cemetery in Edinburgh and was re-interred there.

That was the life and death of Margaret Sinclair or at least the bald facts of that life. Most people who know anything at all of the Venerable Margaret would probably know at least some of these facts. After reading this book readers will discover not only the kind of life she led as a lay person and a religious but above all will realize that although hers was a life lived under the old traditional discipline of church life in those days, Margaret Sinclair, although she lived and died so long before the Second Vatican Council was conceived, nevertheless, unknowingly lived out the general principles emphasized by that Council. In the words of the author: "This makes Margaret Sinclair a particularly appropriate example for Christians today."

The series of books of which this is one of the earliest is particularly concerned with examples of holiness from this century. The Venerable Margaret is, I believe, a prime example of such holiness. Indeed her holiness is already recognized by the fact that she has been declared "Venerable" by the Church. I feel that the book will be welcomed by all devotees of Margaret Sinclair and undoubtedly will attract more people to read about her and be encouraged in their spiritual lives. Most important, readers will realize that everyone is called to holiness, as was Margaret, whatever their walk of life. Every state of life can, and should be, a holy state.

I welcome this little work on the life of the Venerable Margaret and warmly recommend it. My thanks to Felicity O'Brien in compiling it with such care and devotion.

Fr Stephen McGrath OFM
Vice-Postulator

June 1989

1

Margaret: A short biography

Margaret Anne Sinclair was born on 29th March 1900 at 24 Middle Arthur Place, Edinburgh. A few days later, on 11th April, she was taken to the Parish Church of St Patrick and baptized. Her parents, Elizabeth and Andrew, had moved to Edinburgh, from Dundee, in 1897 — the year after their marriage on 1st January 1896. Elizabeth came from a Catholic family and Andrew's conversion to Catholicism a few months before their wedding met with strong disapproval from his family. His first job in Edinburgh was in a tannery. He then became a dustman, working for the city corporation.

Margaret was the third of six Sinclair children who survived infancy. She had an elder brother and sister, John and Isabella (Bella). The three younger children were: Andrew, Elizabeth (Lizzie) and Lawrence.

Childhood

To accommodate their growing family the Sinclairs moved to a three-roomed flat at 13

Blackfriars Street. There Margaret shared a room with her sisters; her brothers shared another room, and her parents slept in the kitchen. There was no bathroom, and the toilet was shared with several other families. The street was in a slum area of the city, with all the grime, noise, and moral and social problems of the Industrial Revolution. Margaret's elder brother, John, later remarked that Blackfriars Street was a place where every commandment was broken. Drunkenness was a common sight and one or two of the houses were brothels.

Margaret certainly knew what material poverty was like in her early life, as she saw her mother scrubbing and cleaning to keep the rooms spotless and tidy, and saw her suffering from depression when the struggle to make ends meet, and the generally dismal surrounding of the area, got her down.

Elizabeth was sometimes tempted to find a "pick-me-up" in alcohol. Margaret used to plead with her gently not to give way to this temptation, and helped her mother to find renewed courage in the face of difficulties. Her mother said that Margaret always understood her worries. With her smile and her ability to understand, Margaret was seen as a ray of sunshine in the home.

Both her parents were strong in their religious faith and did their utmost to see that the children were in no way harmed by the evil influences that flourished outside their home in Blackfriars Street. They regularly attended Mass and the family gathered each evening for prayer. At Christmas, the children were taken to various churches to see the cribs. During the year they visited the churches where the Forty Hours devotion was in progress and the Blessed Sacrament was exposed on the altar. Elizabeth Sinclair encouraged her children to place everything in the hands of Our Lady, assuring them that the Blessed Virgin was always ready to help them.

Margaret received her First Communion and was confirmed in St Patrick's Church on 8th May 1910

She attended St Anne's Catholic School, run by the Sisters of Mercy. Her teachers were unable to recall much about her. One of them described her as a "pale-faced, large-eyed little mouse, with a sweet expression". She was respectful to her teachers and did her best with her schoolwork. Indeed, as she got older, she helped Bella with her work, despite the fact that Bella was two years older. Nevertheless, Margaret was very much an "ordinary" student in her standard of work and in her examination passes.

It was in games that the "large-eyed little mouse" made her mark, winning prizes for running and swimming. She enjoyed games, and her school friends spoke of her as some-one "always laughing and ready for fun".

Her mother recalled that Margaret was particularly good at the game of "Diabolo", in which a double cone is thrown and caught on a cord attached to two sticks. She would get her mother to lean out of the window to see if the cone reached the height of their third-floor flat. In the school playground, Margaret was always anxious to help any child who was unhappy and did all she could to cheer them up.

The Sinclair family was a closely united one. Margaret and Bella were particularly close — sometimes, in fact, they were mis-taken for twins. Margaret used to remark how fortunate they were to be such a happy and united family. "Thank God for a good father and mother," she used to say. She herself contributed a great deal to the family's hap-piness. Although she tended to be quiet and reserved outside the home, when she was with her family she was the life and soul of the party, according to her sister Lizzie: a cheerful and amusing person who enjoyed telling and hearing stories which made her laugh — sometimes until the tears ran down her face.

Margaret's mother described her as obedi-ent and helpful at home, prompt to do what-ever she was asked. She was something of a second mother to Lizzie, who later described herself as having been an awkward child, inclined to speak sharply to people. Margaret told her to count to ten on these occasions as she did not know what harm might be done by speaking like this. Of Margaret, Lizzie said: "She was very kind to the younger members of the family. I never heard her say an angry word to any of us."

However, Margaret was no push-over or doormat, as can be seen from one occasion when she felt that firm words — and actions — were necessary. She disliked undue familiarity and made that clear when a young boy grabbed hold of her exclaiming in jest: "Oh, my little darling." After she had taken the parcel she was carrying into her house, she marched outside again to the boy. When she came back into the house, somewhat flushed and out of breath, she announced: "He won't say that to me again, for I have given him a good lesson." The family couldn't help laughing at her indignant attitude — and she joined in the laughter. Her father used to tease her about the incident and she would smile but insist: "I was quite right."

During her childhood Margaret suffered a number of illnesses: German measles, whooping cough, mumps and pleurisy. She also had attacks of neuralgia which gave her some sleepless nights. She was a good patient and, if ever Bella made a sympathetic comment about Margaret having been kept awake by an attack of neuralgia, Margaret would dismiss it as nothing.

Young adulthood

In her final year at school Margaret had a part-time job, running errands for a shop. But, when the job expanded to include scrubbing and cleaning, it became too tiring and her mother put a stop to it. Although, as a small child, Margaret had talked about becoming a nurse, she in fact became an apprentice French-polisher at the Waverley Cabinet Works when she left school at the age of 14. Along with Bella, she also attended evening classes and obtained certificates in sewing, dressmaking and cookery, from the Atholl Crescent School of Domestic Economy.

Over the nine years from 1914, Margaret worked as a French-polisher in several firms. In 1915, she worked for Scholman's but that job ended when it became difficult to obtain materials because of the war. Her next job, with a firm in Clerk Street, fared no better — the proprietor went bankrupt; again, the problems of war-time were to blame. For three years, Margaret worked at Sheerwinter in the High Street. Then, from 1920-1921, she was employed in the Civil Service Stores in George

Street. Her final post before entering the religious life was with McVitie's & Price.

She was a conscientious worker, much appreciated by her various employers. She cared about her fellow-workers and their conditions of employment. For a time, she belonged to a trade union and did her best to obtain equal pay for women who were doing the same work as the men but getting paid considerably less. However, she was not successful. She decided to resign from a committee to which she had been delegated when she found that meetings were largely occupied by idle chatter. She felt that this waste of time was unjust to the workers who paid the committee members for their services.

Margaret's working day was long — from 8 a.m. to 6 p.m. — and the work itself was hard. Nevertheless, each morning Margaret got up in time to go to Mass and receive Holy Communion. As the Eucharistic Fast was from midnight at that time, she occasionally had to go without breakfast if the priest was late starting the Mass and there was no time to eat before getting the bus to work. She didn't mind making such sacrifices.

Margaret joined various devotional societies such as the Handmaids of the Blessed Sacrament, and the Children of Mary. She repeatedly read and thought about the Scriptures, and enjoyed reading the lives of holy people. Some of these were in books borrowed from various places including a nearby convent where she was a frequent visitor; others were in pamphlets from the Catholic Truth Society stand in the Jesuit Church of the Sacred Heart. Bella would persuade Margaret to read out the stories while she got on with the housework: "You read aloud, Margaret, while I sweep."

The lives included the Scottish martyr, St John Ogilvie (whose sense of humour appealed to Margaret), St Oliver Plunkett and St Gemma Galgani. Sometimes, the reading sessions would go on late into the night — until their father banged on the wall and reminded them that he had to get up very early in the morning.

Margaret's favourite prayers included the Penitential Psalms and the Jesus Psalter. But, she would not recite the prayers requesting that her purgatory should take place on earth because, while she did not mind the thought of suffering for herself, she was afraid it might involve her parents in suffering too. She was particularly attracted by the "Little Way" of St Therese of Lisieux.

Life for Margaret was certainly not all work and no play. At home the family would haul out the gramophone and enjoy sessions of singing and dancing together. When they went to dances arranged by the Caledonians (a Scottish Catholic Society) or to parish socials, Margaret was exuberant, said Lizzie.

She also went to the cinema with Bella and found Charlie Chaplin films hilarious.

One evening Margaret and Bella were invited to a whist drive. They wondered what sort of drive it was. Should they wrap up warmly as it was in the evening? Neither they nor their mother knew anything at all about whist drives. Only when the two sisters arrived at the parish hall did they find out. They saw everyone sitting around tables, in their best clothes. Racing home to change, Margaret and Bella exclaimed to their mother: "It's a party!"

The family finances improved as the children grew up and went out to work. Among other things, it meant that Margaret and Bella were able to afford an annual holiday. The first place they went to was Dundee where they had relatives. In the following years they went to Rosewell, Bo'ness and Loch Lomond. Margaret's favourite holiday was at Rosewell. Opportunities for silence were few at their home in Edinburgh and yet Margaret was drawn to silence and meditation. It is little wonder then that she relished that holiday in a small cottage in the country. The sound of birds and of wind rustling the leaves replaced the clatter of traffic and all the cacophony of crowded inner-city life. Margaret relished the countryside: "How lovely it is here, away from all the noise of the world and all its temptations," she said to Bella.

It was on the Rosewell holiday that Margaret persuaded Bella to join her in going each day to Mass and Communion. The daily reception of Holy Communion was still not common practice then and Bella expressed some doubts about her own worthiness. Margaret quickly reassured her: "You are not going because you are good, but because you want to try to be good." She assured Bella that once she began to go to daily Mass and Communion she wouldn't be able to live without it.

The priest who was supplying at Rosewell at that time remembered seeing the two sisters at Mass each day:

"From the beginning of my stay I had noticed two girls, obviously sisters, attending church very regularly, both at Penicuik and Rosewell. I took more notice of them from the fact that the distance between the two places was about five miles, as far as I remember, and the other fact that the weather all that week was extremely wet and unseasonable."

The priest was impressed by their "quiet and modest piety", and decided to call them into the sacristy after Mass on the last morning. There he exhorted them to continue their practice of daily Mass and Communion.

"In outward appearance the two girls were very refined. I thought they were teachers, or boarders at a convent, if I thought anything.

They were well dressed, both alike, in dark blue coats. But it was their interior radiance which shone out through their exterior features that made an impression which still lasts."

Two years after the Rosewell holiday, Margaret and Bella went to stay in Bo'ness on the Firth of Forth. It was during this holiday that Margaret met a young ex-serviceman, Patrick Lynch, who was also an ex-practising Catholic. Margaret wanted to bring him back to the practice of his religion and accepted his invitation to go out with him — provided that Bella went along too. Margaret succeeded in persuading him to go to Mass with them and also got him to promise to try and give up the habit of using the Holy Name as an exclamation. She told him it was painful for her to hear him use the name irreverently.

Drawn to Margaret, Patrick did his utmost to amend his ways. In fact, he became an exemplary Catholic who would later say that Margaret had made a new man of him. However, the attraction was only one-sided and Margaret, while she had been deeply concerned for Patrick's spiritual welfare — particularly as there was anti-Catholic feeling where he was living — felt nothing more. Unfortunately, he would not take "no" for an answer and refused to take seriously her firm statements that she would not marry him; nor was he put off by her obvious coolness towards him. He continued to hope against hope.

Margaret's parents liked the young man and her mother said he would make a good husband. He came to be seen as almost one of the family. Bella used to tease him and he took it all in good part. Margaret made the mistake of accepting Patrick's offer to buy her a ring which they saw in a shop window, on her birthday. She accepted it to please him, but she saw it simply as a "dress" ring and said so in front of Patrick and her parents that same evening. In fact, over the following months, she rarely wore the ring. However, it soon became clear that Patrick regarded the ring and her acceptance of it as tantamount to an official engagement.

Margaret found herself in an extremely difficult and painful situation. She told a friend that she had only gone out with him in order to bring him back to the Church. And, later, Patrick was to say that their conversations had been mostly about religion. The influence she had been able to bring to bear on Patrick regarding the practice of his faith, and the fact that her family liked him so much and would be disappointed if she did not marry him, made Margaret wonder whether it was God's will that she should marry him. Not wishing to disappoint her family, she hoped that she might come to like Patrick and prayed that God would make her love him if the marriage was what God willed.

The months drifted on, with no improvement in Margaret's feelings towards Patrick. She would permit no such familiarity as walking arm-in-arm, and she refused to go out alone with him. When members of her family reproached her for her coolness towards Patrick, she said she could not be otherwise. She had told Patrick that she did not wish to marry him, and had even written to him telling him this, but he simply turned up to see why she had written in this way. Eventually, her mother advised her to be completely frank with him and make a final break as she was evidently so unhappy at the prospect of marrying him.

Margaret decided to put the whole matter to a priest, Fr Thomas Agius, SJ, and get his advice: would it be wrong for her to break the "engagement"? After listening to her, the priest told her she was not bound to marry Patrick.

Greatly relieved, Margaret wrote to Patrick, telling him that she really did wish to break with him because she did not care for him. She continued: "I have done what God inspired me to do, to help you the little I could to regain the Light. From that moment, God and his Blessed Mother must have showered down their blessings on you, because you have remained steadfast since, and I trust in God that you will continue doing so, because you know he is the only real happiness."

She reminded him that she had written a similar letter a year before but that he had come and implored her not to make the break.

"I must be rather chicken-hearted, because I agreed, but I feel I cannot let it go on any longer. Perhaps you will be hurt at my saying this, but if you take a broad view of it you will see it is better now than after."

Margaret had made the final break but Patrick later said that even after Margaret had entered the convent he hoped she would come out again and marry him.

Vocation

Margaret had long admired the religious life but, whenever there was any mention of the possibility of her entering a convent, she would comment that she could never get up early enough in the mornings. However, as she got older the idea began to grow. Shortly before she broke off her "engagement" with Patrick, she had said to Bella: "I should like to enter a convent. I have seen something of life in the world, and though I have enjoyed it I do not think much of it. I do not think it is for me."

Bella was also considering a religious vocation. Fr Agius, to whom Margaret, Bella and a friend, regularly went to confession, had asked each of them if they had considered such a vocation. The friend mentioned this to Margaret and Bella and they said that the question had also been put to them.

Margaret felt herself being drawn towards the religious life, and also did much to encourage Bella to follow her vocation. Bella decided to join the Little Sisters of the Poor. The Poor Clare Colettines was the Order on which Margaret set her heart. Her decision seemed to be finally taken after hearing a priest talk in the church about the Poor Clares and their poverty. Afterwards, a collection was taken up for them. Margaret was deeply moved by the priest's words and Lizzie said it was the only time she had seen Margaret in tears.

She spoke to Fr Agius about her hopes of entering the Poor Clares. He was frank about the difficulties of such a life, but Margaret was undeterred. Although she had, in the past, expressed the view that she would not live long as she was not particularly strong, she was convinced that, if God was giving her this vocation, he would also give her ample strength.

For Elizabeth Sinclair the prospect of seeing two of her daughters go into convents was a heavy blow, especially as their younger brother, Andrew, was going to Canada. But she told them: "Go where God calls you."

When Elizabeth learnt that both Margaret and Bella wished to enter convents, she went with them to an early morning Mass and, at the Consecration, said: "My God, if you wish, take them, and make me worthy. I give them to you."

She, like several friends when they learnt of the two sisters' decision, asked them why they didn't join the same Order. It would have seemed the natural thing for them to do as they were so close. However, Margaret and Bella not only felt drawn towards their respective Orders but considered that it would not be a real sacrifice if they both joined the same one.

Bella joined the Little Sisters of the Poor in June 1923. Margaret and her mother accompanied her to the convent. Her mother was reluctant to leave. Margaret sat with her in the garden until she felt better and then took her home. Margaret had wondered whether she should delay her own entry into the Poor Clares so that her mother did not have to "lose" her two elder daughters at once, but Fr Agius had felt that it would be better not to prolong the process by delaying her entry. Margaret followed his advice.

She had applied to the Poor Clares Convent at Liberton to be admitted as an extern sister — she did not think she was good enough to join the enclosed choir nuns. As there were already four girls waiting to enter there as extern sisters, Margaret was advised to apply to the convent at Notting Hill, London. She did so and was accepted.

When Margaret gave in her notice at work, her employers tried to persuade her to stay. As an incentive, they offered her a rise in wages. They also offered to keep her job open for her to return to after a holiday she had planned to take, before entering the convent, in order to get over a cough that had been troubling her.

None of this meant anything to Margaret who had her sights firmly set on the Poor Clares at Notting Hill. She went off to a convalescence home run by the Sisters of Charity, at Lanark. On her return home, the doctor who examined her declared that she was fit for her chosen way of life.

And so, in July 1923 — a month after Bella had entered the Little Sisters of the Poor — Margaret set off for London. Family and friends accompanied her to the station. She was travelling with her brother Andrew and going to see him onto the ship which was taking him to Canada.

Margaret's elder brother, John, recalled that she was all smiles, but there were tears among the family and friends. "This is goodbye, Margaret," said one person. "No, it isn't goodbye. We shall meet in heaven," she replied. To add to the emotion of the moment, some sailors, further up the train, be-

27

gan singing "Auld Lang Syne". Finally they were off, on the long over-night journey to London.

The following day they went to Westminster Cathedral, where they received Holy Communion. They then visited some of the sights in London. Andrew had arranged to stay the night in a hotel and Margaret stayed with the Sisters of Charity whose convent was near to the Poor Clares. (If she had gone immediately to the Poor Clares, she would not have been able to see Andrew off the following day.)

On 21st July Margaret went with Andrew to Tilbury Docks. As soon as she had seen him onto his ship, Margaret went to the Poor Clares Convent. The annual retreat was in progress there. Normally, postulants were not admitted at such a time but an exception had been made in Margaret's case so that she could travel to London with her brother.

The Mother Abbess received her in the parlour and placed her in the care of the sister in charge of the extern sisters. In the afternoon, she wrote a brief note to her parents to let them know that she had arrived safely. She told them not to worry about her, that she was very well, and that, although they were far apart, they would be reunited every evening at the time of the family rosary.

Later in the day, while getting on with some sewing she had been given to do, Margaret's emotions overwhelmed her and she wept for a long time. It is not difficult to imagine something of what she must have been feeling. The previous month she had said goodbye to Bella who had been her closest friend and confidante for many years; she had said goodbye to her parents, other members of the family, and friends; she had left all that was familiar, in her home and the city of Edinburgh; she had left her homeland of Scotland; and, finally, she had just said goodbye to Andrew, the brother of whom she was so fond. In addition, she had just embarked on a different way of life.

To the consternation of the sister in charge, Margaret suddenly went missing. She was soon found — with the priest who was conducting the retreat in the convent. He had come across the new postulant in tears, and had taken her back to his sitting-room to give her some consoling words. It was not long before Margaret was once again her cheerful self, and was given permission to follow some of the retreat meditations.

Religious life

Margaret Sinclair's life as a postulant was not seen by those around her to contain anything remarkable. She was found to be pleasant to live with, cheerful at recreation with

29

jokes and amusing stories to tell the other sisters, and she carried out with great care the work that was given to her. The Mother Abbess was to say later that, from the beginning, Margaret had struck her as being completely good and humble.

Margaret's letters reflected her happiness at being in the convent. In one letter to her family, she enclosed a photograph which showed the plot of ground that she had been given to tend. It included a forlorn apple tree that perked up and blossomed in due season after Margaret had helped to care for it. On the photo, she had marked the window of the room or "cell" which she occupied, saying: "It is the sweetest place imaginable. How I love it."

Writing to Fr Agius she expressed her happiness, and also her amusement at various aspects of life in the convent. "If you only knew all the quaint things we have to do on account of Holy Poverty, you would laugh outright."

On 11th February 1924 — the feast of Our Lady of Lourdes — Margaret received the habit of the Order. The previous September, she had written to her parents saying how much she was looking forward to this event. Her parents and her elder brother, John, came down from Edinburgh for the occasion. Normally, as Margaret was on retreat immediately before the ceremony, they would not have been able to see her beforehand. However, as they had to return to Edinburgh more or less straight after the ceremony, they were given permission to see her the previous evening.

Margaret was having a meal when she heard their voices outside. Try as she might, she was unable to eat another thing because of her excitement at the thought of seeing them again. She was given permission to leave the room, and the joyful reunion took place. Margaret, vivacious and happy, showed her mother the special cake sent for the occasion by a well-wisher in Scotland. She was particularly delighted with this sign of affection from the homeland she loved.

The following day, as Margaret waited in bridal white for the ceremony to begin, she was overjoyed at the arrival of Bella. Bella was in London, on her way to her Order's novitiate in France, and had received permission from her superiors to attend her sister's "clothing".

The chapel was full and Margaret looked radiant as she received not only the habit but also her name in religious life — Sister Mary Francis of the Five Wounds. Now, her year as a novice began.

Like her time as a postulant, her life as a novice was not seen as being in any way extraordinary. She was regarded as just a good novice. The Mother Abbess had commented to the family that if they knew of any other Scottish girls, like Margaret, she would be pleased to have them in the convent. However, when asked, later, about her conversations with Margaret, the Mother Abbess said: "I don't remember anything about our conversations. She was so ordinary that nothing has remained in my memory."

In one letter to her mother Margaret wrote: "In the convent you have your little ups and downs." Life in a monastery or convent is no more all sweetness and light than in any other walk of life. Any community has its mixture of human temperaments, clashes of personality, and misunderstandings.

It is possible to glimpse something of Margaret's "downs" and to see them as being due more to misunderstanding and personal dislike on the part of some of those around her rather than to real faults on her part.

While it was admitted that she did everything she was asked, she was seen by some as being slow, languid, even lazy in her work. Such criticisms appear to lack understanding of both her character and her previous work experience. She was naturally careful and patient over her work. Her mother had always reminded her that, if a thing was worth doing, it was worth doing well. This had stood her in good stead during her nine years of working as a French-polisher which called for painstaking care rather than speed.

There was one occasion when Margaret was regarded as lacking in obedience towards her superiors. This came during a celebration to mark the anniversary of the Mother Abbess's profession. For this, permission was given for the extern sisters to enter the enclosure and join the choir nuns.

During the meal the Mother Abbess asked Margaret to stand up and tell them of some event regarding the outside world which would be of interest to the sisters.

Margaret stood up but remained silent. The Mother Abbess repeated the request but still Margaret said nothing. She was then told that if she did not wish to do as she was told she had better sit down. Margaret sat down. She gave no explanation for her silence.

Later, when questioned about this incident, in connection with Margaret's Cause for possible canonization, the Mother Abbess said she thought that Margaret had probably been nervous as it was the first time she had been in the enclosed part of the convent, and that this had made her tongue-tied. The Mother Abbess felt that if Margaret had, indeed, been a saint then she would not have been nervous!

Fr Agius, who had known Margaret well before she entered the Poor Clares, put forward the theory that Margaret may have been in a state of ecstasy and therefore incapable of speaking, and that, in her humility, she had made no excuse for herself afterwards.[1]

In writing home about the celebrations Margaret certainly appeared to have been overwhelmed by the occasion — although she said nothing about the incident involving her so-called disobedience. She wrote:

"I never experienced such joy as to be present when our Mother Abbess renewed her vows. The Blessed Sacrament being exposed all the time, and the clear voice of Mother Abbess sounding her vows to God; the heavenliness of it all. One could imagine Our Blessed Lord and Our Lady smiling down, and all the choirs of angels rejoicing. I shall never forget that day, it was so good of Our Blessed Lord to allow poor wee me to be present."

Margaret's reserved nature led to her being underestimated. Whenever asked to do something, she would reply: "I will try." She did not put herself forward, or say anything about all the things she was capable of doing. One of the consequences of this was that she was given the most menial tasks to do — but did them cheerfully.

---

[1] There could be a further possible explanation: that the incident was neither a failure to obey nor a failure to speak, but an indication that Margaret in fact found nothing of interest – to herself or to her sisters – in the outside world, but only in the kingdom within. She therefore obeyes the instruction to recount something of interest about the outside world – by remaining silent.

Neither the Mother Abbess, whom Margaret, as an extern sister, did not see very often, nor the sister in charge of the extern sisters seemed to have made any real effort to get to know more about Margaret. Nevertheless, Margaret had a great respect for her superiors and, at one point, mentioned her fears to Fr Agius that her love for her convent might be regarded as excessive.

As an extern sister Margaret's duties included regularly going out with another sister to visit various firms and offices to beg for offerings for the convent. It was not a job to be relished. At best it was embarrassing, at worst it could be humiliating. However, Margaret carried out the task willingly and was remembered for her smile.

One sister, who considered that Margaret did not have the spirit of their Order, said that she had no admiration for her and, in fact, was pleased when Margaret was sent to the sanatorium after contracting tuberculosis, because it meant she would no longer have to be annoyed by her! However, in giving her deposition on oath before the Tribunal set up to gather evidence for the Cause of Margaret Sinclair, she had to leave aside any personal dislike and the result was, in fact, a very positive picture.

She said she had never known Margaret to transgress a commandment of either God or the Church, and that she had practised all the virtues. The sister believed that Margaret had entered the religious life out of pure love of God; that she was united to the will of God; and that she accepted the deprivations arising from religious poverty, for the love of God.

Another sister recalled that Margaret was always cheerful. She did not ever remember her being depressed or in any way unpleasant, nor ever hear her complain. She remembered that there was one sister with whom it was difficult at times to carry on a conversation but that Margaret had always seemed able to find the right word to keep the peace. She was never discourteous, nor was she ever heard making any criticism of her superiors. Margaret's spirit seems, in fact, to have been very much a Franciscan one of joy and love of poverty, such as one would expect of a member of the Poor Clares.

During her novitiate Margaret suffered the loss of her father. News of his death, in an accident, came on 28th December 1924. The Mother Abbess called her into the parlour to tell her what had happened. Margaret received the news with outward calm. After speaking to her for a while, the Mother Abbess told her to go to the crib and place this cross at the feet of the Infant Jesus. A little while later, on receiving a letter from her mother speaking of the difficulties she was now facing following her bereavement, Margaret cried. How she must have longed to help! However, she was consoled when she heard that her mother had received compensation for the death of her husband, thereby alleviating the financial difficulties.

On 14th February 1925 Margaret made her religious profession. No members of her family were able to be present, because of her father's death. But, her smile, commented on afterwards by friends, showed the inner joy she felt at making her profession. At the part of the ceremony where she was required to sing, another sister had been appointed to sing with her as Margaret was tone-deaf and, despite careful practice, could not stay on the right notes.

Physical suffering

Before the ceremony Margaret had mentioned having a sore throat. She was given something for this, but she seemed to remain slightly unwell, lacking in some of her usual fervour as she entered the retreat which preceded her profession.

In the days after the ceremony she still seemed unwell and it was thought that it was probably a reaction to the stress of the ceremony and belated shock at the death of her father. The Mother Abbess told her to stay in bed for a few days, but there was no improvement and a doctor was consulted. He prescribed a gargle for her throat. Some time later, Margaret developed a cough which nothing could alleviate.

Early in March she said that her throat was more painful and she had lost some blood. It was then discovered that she was suffering from tuberculosis of the throat, and it was recommended that she should be sent to the sanatorium, run by the Sisters of Charity of St Vincent de Paul, at Warley in Essex.

Margaret left for Warley on 9th April 1925. It was Holy Thursday and, after taking her leave of the Mother Abbess, she visited the Altar of Repose where she shed a few tears. She had already left her family and her homeland but it was in order to achieve her heart's desire of joining the Poor Clares. Now, within a short time of being professed, she had to leave her convent for the sanatorium. It was an enormous wrench, even though she was prepared to accept whatever God's will might be for her.

Two of the extern sisters accompanied her on the journey. On the way to the station, Margaret shed more tears but then remained calm and quiet. The two sisters stayed with her for a while at the sanatorium. Margaret was once again her cheerful self — although there were some more tears when the two sisters had to leave.

During the seven months she was at Warley Margaret was considered anything but ordinary. She was regarded as a saint by the nursing sisters and visitors alike. She had much to suffer including breathlessness, choking, vomiting and a racking cough, but she never complained and showed no sign of the irritability which can accompany such sufferings.

When her mother and brother, John, visited her soon after she arrived there, they found her in good spirits, although, shortly before, she had been sufficiently ill to receive the Last Sacraments. When she later wrote to them, the letter was full of interest in the family and what they were up to. At the end, she spoke of her gratitude for all that was being done for her.

The illness was painful enough in itself but, on one occasion, during a coughing fit, a wasp flew into her mouth and stung her throat. The sister who was looking after her at the time asked herself why such a thing should have happened to someone who was already suffering so much. But Margaret, once over the initial shock, smiled and simply said that it was "only another wee splinter of the cross". The same sister said that Margaret never thought of herself, only of others. Each day she would ask how the other patients were getting on.

She did not lose her sense of humour. When a new patient arrived one day, Margaret was told that her name was Sister Clare.

Margaret promptly said that she was the only lady there. After a brief pause, and some puzzled looks, she continued: "You are all Bernards, or Johns, or Columbas." (Margaret herself was, of course, a "Francis".)

Margaret's cough was so bad that she had to be moved to various parts of the sanatorium so that she didn't disturb other patients. After the sixth move, she tearfully expressed the hope that that would be the last move, but she still managed a smile. She offered all her pain, in union with Christ, for the salvation of souls. If a particularly painful day came along, she was pleased, saying that it was worth it if just one soul could be saved.

The chaplain at the sanatorium said:

"My frequent visits to her always impressed and uplifted me. She was very spiritual but she had a keen sense of humour, and up to the last she thoroughly enjoyed a good joke."

She gave no indication of likes and dislikes and never asked for anything. However, she showed great delight when an apple from "her" tree at the convent was brought along and cooked for her, and when some grapes were brought in she exclaimed that God was so good to her — he sent her everything she wished for.

The books she loved best during her illness were the New Testament and the *Imitation of Christ*. In the latter, she liked most the chapters: "Of the love of Jesus above all things", "Of familiar friendship with Jesus", and "Of the wonderful effects of Divine Love" (Chapters 7 and 8 of Book II and Chapter 5 of Book III).

One of the sisters who looked after her said: "She always seemed to live in the presence of God, yet she never made a show of holiness. Indeed, it was her great reserve that impressed me most, together with her humility and charity. Never once did I hear her say an uncharitable word, and she was so grateful for even the smallest services."

She faced death calmly. She spoke of her Requiem Mass and of the joys of heaven. Her only concern seemed to be that she should have her habit on when she was dying and that she should have a copy of her vows, her crucifix and blessed candle to hand, ready to greet the Divine Bridegroom.

On the night she died she whispered short prayers asking God's forgiveness and commending her soul to Jesus, to the Blessed Virgin and to St Joseph, patron of a happy death. She died at 4.45 a.m. on 24th November 1925. The gentle smile remained even in death.

Her body was taken back to the Poor Clares Convent in London in the early evening of the same day, and placed in the convent chapel. Her burial took place at Kensal Green Cemetery which was covered in a white mantle of snow. Just a few people were present: a priest, a handful of nuns from the Poor Clares, the Sisters of Charity, and the Little Sisters of the Poor. It was surely as Margaret would have liked it: peaceful, quiet, simple.

Canonization process

As interest in Margaret Sinclair grew, it was decided to move her body from Kensal Green Cemetery back to her home city of Edinburgh. On 20th December 1927 the exhumation took place.

The coffin was taken by train to Edinburgh and buried in Mount Vernon Cemetery. The name plate had fallen off her coffin but proof that it was Margaret's was found in the form of a scrap of paper which was all that remained of the written formula of her vows, which had been buried with her. Sufficient remained of it to give the name: "Sr Mary Francis of the Five Wounds".

In the summer of 1930 the first step was taken towards the possible canonization of Margaret Sinclair: the Informative Process — in which evidence was taken from those who had known Margaret. The evidence gathered was then sent to Rome. Nine years later another stage was reached: her writings were approved. In 1942 Pope Pius XII signed the official Introduction of her Cause into the

Sacred Congregation of Rites (now the Sacred Congregation for the Causes of the Saints). In 1978 it was solemnly declared that Margaret had practised the virtues to a heroic degree.

2

Margaret: the cheerful giver

What was it that particularly struck people about Margaret Sinclair? What was the "keynote" of her life, of her spirituality? The word so often used to describe her was "cheerful". She was, indeed, noted for her smile, but this outer cheerfulness can be seen as coming from something much deeper — a wholehearted embracing of God's will and a great spirit of generosity towards God, her family, friends, acquaintances — and strangers.

Definitions of the word "cheerful" in the dictionary include: bright, contented, hopeful, and willing. Margaret was all those things but, especially she was *willing* — willing to help everyone, willing to do her best, willing to give. She provides an outstanding example of what St Paul was talking about when he said: "He who sows bountifully will also reap bountifully. Each one must do as he has made up his mind, not reluctantly or under compulsion, for God loves a cheerful giver" (2 Cor 9:6-7).

Margaret showed the simplicity, the practicality, of living out this aspect of the Gospel; of following, with a radical spirit of generosity, in the footsteps of Christ who was the cheerful giver *par excellence*.

Her example makes it clear that to be a cheerful giver in the service of God and neighbour it is not necessary to have an abundance of the world's goods, nor to have exceptional talents and abilities. It is primarily an attitude of mind towards God and towards other people; an attitude that makes us generous in whatever ways may be available to us in our particular lives.

The deprived inner-city area in which Margaret grew up might seem an unlikely place to find any kind of cheerfulness or generosity flourishing. What was there to be cheerful about? How could someone be generous when it was a struggle to make ends meet?

Margaret certainly did not sail through her childhood and youth with her head in the clouds. She knew at first-hand all about poverty and hard work; she saw and heard the effects all around her, in her house and in the neighbourhood. She saw her mother weighed down at times by depression; she saw her father come home worn-out after a day that began around 5 a.m. Nevertheless, Margaret was cheerful in every respect, and she found plenty of ways to be generous.

Cheerfulness in its various aspects should be a characteristic of every Christian. It abounds in the New Testament. The stories in the Gospels, surrounding Christ's birth, are full of cheerfulness.

There is the hope-filled announcement to Mary that she had been chosen to be the Mother of Christ; there is her whole-hearted, willing response. The meeting between Mary and her cousin, Elizabeth, could hardly have been portrayed in brighter tones. The message of hope given to the shepherds on the night of Christ's birth evoked prompt action: "'Let us go over to Bethlehem and see this thing that has happened, which the Lord has made known to us.' And they went with haste..." (Lk 2:15-16).

Similarly, there was no sign of reluctance on the part of the wise men from the East as they journeyed to find the new King. In the Temple, Simeon can be seen as contentment personified as he held the child in his arms and declared: "Lord, now lettest thou thy servant depart in peace, according to thy word; for mine eyes have seen thy salvation which thou hast prepared in the presence of all peoples, a light for revelation to the Gentiles, and for the glory to thy people Israel" (Lk 2:29-32).

And what of Christ's preaching? In the Sermon on the Mount he reached out to those who mourned, those who longed for righteousness, those who were persecuted for the cause of righteousness, and gave them the bright hope that all would be well in the end, no matter how dark things might be appear.

Something of the attitude that Christ expected of his followers can be seen in his words: "When you fast, do not look dismal, like the hypocrites..." (Mt 6:16). Before leaving his apostles to go to his death on the cross Christ told them: "In the world you have tribulation; but be of good cheer, I have overcome the world" (Jn 16:33). And the greatest message of cheer that the world has ever heard is: "He is risen."

Contentment is an aspect of cheerfulness about which St Paul had something to say: "I have learned, in whatever state I am, to be content. I know how to be abased, and I know how to abound; in any and all circumstances I have learned the secret of facing plenty and hunger, abundance and want. I can do all things in him who strengthens me" (Ph 4:11-13)

No matter what odds are stacked against them, whatever trials they encounter, there is a light-heartedness about those who keep close to Christ, because they know they are not alone. They seize life with both hands and live it to the full — not by "taking" but by "giving"; not by amassing fortunes or squandering their time in one frivolous activity after another, but by living in and with the risen Christ.

For them, Christ is not just an historical figure, nor a faint image at the back of their minds, brought out for Sundays and occasions of special need, but a powerful, vital reality in their lives. They hear the Word of God and prove to be the good soil which "bears fruit, and yields, in one case a hundredfold, in another sixty, and in another thirty" (Mt 13:23). The Christian knows that Christ is with him or her and that he or she cannot, in fact, function alone: "Apart from me you can do nothing" (Jn 15:5).

As Margaret grew up in the Edinburgh slums she inevitably faced the problems and frustrations to be encountered in such an environment, but she was a truly contented person. The natural cheerfulness and willingness to help that were apparent in her as a toddler gradually matured and developed into an ever more generous spirit of willing self-sacrifice and generous acceptance of all that she saw to be God's will for her.

Generosity is not dependent on material wealth. A person with plenty of worldly goods and a healthy bank balance may give away large amounts and yet still not have a spirit of generosity whereas someone with few possessions and very little money can, nevertheless, be a person of immense generosity. One has only to think of Christ's praise of the widow who put two copper coins into the Temple treasury while richer people were putting in large amounts: "Truly, I say to you, this poor widow has put in more than all those who are contributing to the treasury. For they all contributed out of their abundance; but she out of her poverty has put in everything she had, her whole living" (Mk 12:43-44).

Generosity goes far beyond a financial aspect. It applies also to such things as time and talents. Margaret was generous with her time, whether it was helping in the home, writing letters for a neighbour, visiting the sick, or helping one or other of her sisters with their school-work. She was generous with her talents. Among these was needle-work which was put to good use in the family and, as she got older, for helping to mend vestments and altar linen. After she had left school and become a French-polisher she was happy to volunteer her skills in this direction.

Some people have looked at the things Margaret did and said: "Is that all?" Yes, that was "all" in its simplicity — and yet, because of the way she did those simple things, it was "everything". Only someone who had never tried to live as she did could say: "Is that all?"

It is relatively easy to be generous — towards God and towards those around us — for some, even much [most?] of the time. Heroism comes into it when the giving, of ourselves and what we have, is continually done, in season and out of season, no matter how we may personally feel. It becomes

50

Christian heroism when it is done for the love of Christ.

The next three chapters look at some of the ways in which Margaret lived a life of cheerful giving — to her family, her neighbours, and to God.

3

Generosity in the family

Many young children delight in helping around the home, fascinated by the humdrum tasks that, to them, look so grown-up. This early enthusiasm tends to wear off and it is not long before parents are having to make repeated and ever stronger calls to their off-spring to make their beds, tidy their room, or give a hand with the dishes. If the calls are heeded, it is often with considerable reluctance. Margaret was noticeably different.

As a toddler Margaret used to say to her mother, "I wish I was a big girl so I could help you." Help she did, as soon as she was able, and she went on helping, more and more, through her childhood and into adolescence and adulthood. Her mother said she always preferred to ask Margaret to do something, rather than one of the other children, because she was so willing. Margaret would say to her mother: "Don't *ask* me, *tell* me to do it!" If she happened to be playing a game when asked to do something, she would stop at once in order to do whatever was required.

As the children grew up each was given particular tasks in the home. Margaret looked after one of the three rooms and also the staircase leading to their flat. Bella's responsibility was for the kitchen, and Lizzie kept the third room and the hall clean. The job of cleaning the stairs was one that Margaret would not let anyone else do because it was particularly dirty and tiring work. (She also cleaned the stairs for any neighbours who were ill or elderly.) Whenever more than one job needed doing, Margaret would let the others have first choice or choose the most difficult one for herself.

Margaret was not only prompt in doing what she was asked and willing to take on the most disagreeable jobs but was also quick to anticipate needs. This was something she also encouraged in her brothers and sisters. To Andrew she said: "You shouldn't need telling to do things by mother. She has had a hard day. You should do it without being told." Her brother, John, said of her: "Margaret was truly an example for us and encouraged us to be quick to obey without having to be asked twice to do something."

It didn't mean, of course, that she always relished the jobs she had to do. Being a cheerful giver doesn't mean always actually *liking* the things undertaken. On Friday evenings, when she had the job of cleaning the brass in the household, Margaret used to say that when she had a house of her own she wouldn't have anything made of brass.

Another task which invariably fell to her but gave her no great cause for rejoicing was the writing of letters for the family. During the war years she was the one who had to write to her father and elder brother, John, who had been called up, to tell them the family news. Sometimes it was hard to think what to say. Grammar and spelling were not Margaret's strong points and her punctuation — or the lack of it — caused some amusement. Her father teased her about the time she wrote on behalf of her mother (who could not read or write) ending the letter with "God keep you from your loving wife". She had not seen that a full stop was required after "God keep you" in order to give the meaning actually intended.

Lizzie who, looking back, thought she must have been a real cross for Margaret, said that, until she had children of her own, she had thought that the way in which Margaret had treated her was the way in which all elder sisters treated their younger brothers and sisters!

She recalled: "She was like a second mother to me; her gentle ways made me love her. I always looked upon her as older than Bella, for she was less impulsive and seemed more experienced in her ways."

Whenever her mother was especially busy, Margaret willingly undertook the task of getting Lizzie up in the morning, washing and dressing her. At school she would make sure that Lizzie kept warm in the playground, getting her to run about. This meant a quiet sacrifice for Margaret who was good at games and enjoyed playing with friends of her own age but she didn't show any reluctance in her care for the child. Margaret's own cheerfulness was something she tried to pass on to her younger sister. She frequently reminded her to look cheerful at all times because a cheerful face made other people happy.

Margaret's younger brother, Andrew, thought the world of her and happily followed her around wherever she went with Bella. The latter was none too keen on having their little brother trailing after them but Margaret would say: "Poor wee soul. He has no one to play with. Let him come with us." If either Lizzie or Andrew asked Margaret to take them for a walk she would happily oblige. It is not surprising that, in later years, Lizzie said of her: "She was very kind with the younger members of the family", and that Andrew described her as "always good and kind to us at home".

Margaret helped both Bella and Lizzie with school-work. Lizzie's teacher remarked that she wished all elder sisters were like Margaret. When she was a child Margaret liked to save up the half-pennies she was given to buy some small gift for her parents at Christmas, or a hair-ribbon for Lizzie. When she and

Bella had left school and were at work they used to buy small treats for the family — chocolates or sweets.

Even before she left school Margaret was eager to help with the family finances by taking on a part-time job running errands. She didn't complain when the work began to include cleaning stairs and floors but her mother saw that she was getting very tired and put a stop to it. When she did go out to full-time employment Margaret handed over her wage-packets to her mother and had just a small amount of pocket money.

Home and family life provide an abundance of opportunities to be a cheerful giver, and Margaret took advantage of them all.

Home is where people are seen "warts and all"; a place to relax and be completely at ease; where it is not necessary to worry about what others think. There can, of course, be disadvantages as well as advantages in this. It is in the home, particularly, that there is the tendency not to hold back the sharp word, not make a real effort to shake off a mood of depression; indeed, sometimes to be thoroughly unpleasant while keeping a smile and a polite word for the stranger. There is a verse that runs:

"We have careful thought for the stranger,
And smiles for the sometime guest;
But for our own, the bitter tone,
Though we love our own the best."

If this tendency is true of many homes for at least some of the time, how much more is it the case in crowded conditions in a thoroughly run-down area. Everyone likes room to breathe and the lack of it causes tension. From her earliest years Margaret lived in conditions which provided ample opportunity for the exercise of patience on the part of all concerned, not least by Margaret herself.

She had a naturally quick temper and mastered it only by determined vigilance and frequently turning to the Lord for help. As she got older she told Bella that the only way she could stop herself saying something she might regret was to say a short prayer or inwardly repeat the name of Jesus. Sometimes, she resorted to leaving the room for a while — returning shortly afterwards, with a smile, having regained her composure. She was also seen as the peacemaker in the family. John said that she was "good at making peace at home if one of us got angry". She knew how to throw in a humorous remark to defuse the situation.

Margaret and Bella were very close but there were, on occasions, disputes between them. Margaret was the first to apologize even when Bella was wrong. When Bella asked her why she did that Margaret said good-humouredly: "One of us had to make an act of humility!"

To control her own impatience and to act

as a peacemaker involved Margaret in unspectacular but nonetheless real self-discipline and self-denial. In these ways, too, Margaret proved to be quietly and consistently the cheerful giver.

The family saw her as someone completely reliable to whom they could turn for help or advice. Bella, although older than Margaret, often asked her advice. Margaret was regarded as discreet and understanding. They knew that she would not discuss family affairs outside the home.

She was happy to put herself out for others. When her future sister-in-law began to take instruction in the faith Margaret willingly arranged to meet her and accompany her because she knew the young woman was nervous about going to see the priest. However, when the time came Margaret had influenza and it meant getting out of bed and going out in the snow to meet her. To make matters worse, the young woman was delayed and Margaret had to wait in the icy cold for her but she made no complaint and remained cheerful as ever, dismissing the apologies, saying it was nothing. Needless to say, Margaret's influenza was not improved by this snowy venture but she considered it all worthwhile because it was helping someone come closer to God.

Margaret's cheerfulness and willingness to help in any way she could extended well beyond her family and it is her relationships with friends, and with neighbours in the broadest scriptural sense of the word, that will be looked at in the next chapter.

4

The neighbourly saint

"You can't help them all, Margaret", her elder brother, John said to her but she certainly tried. Her mother said that Margaret would have gone anywhere to do a good deed. A friend said that the only ambition that Margaret seemed to have was to be kind and helpful to others. She gave her help on two fronts — materially and spiritually.

"I will pray for you", she would often say to people. She had an abundant trust in God and her first response to anyone in difficulty was to tell them she would pray for them. This was no idle promise but something she really meant. Each day she made her morning offering and included in her intentions those whom she knew needed her prayers.

Neighbours for Margaret were those close at hand — in the same building, the same street; those in more distant parts of the city; those in foreign lands; and the Holy Souls. They included people whom she knew well and those who would remain personally unknown to her in this life.

Her generous, out-going spirit was evident in childhood not only in her behaviour at home but in the way she acted towards other children. One small example concerns the use of a swing — something of a luxury commodity in the area.

Margaret and her brothers and sisters had access to one and other children used to gather to watch enviously. Margaret was always the first to suggest that they give each of the children twenty "swings" in order to make them happy. She wanted to share her enjoyment whether it was swings, or the sweets which occasionally came her way.

Bella noticed that Margaret never tried to get her own way when she was playing with her friends. Whenever she won games or races she made sure that others won subsequent ones. If she was playing with something that someone else wanted she was quick to give it up.

As she got older she gave increasing help to those in the neighbourhood who were in any kind of need. Both she and Bella used to visit the sick. John's wife, Helen, said: "Margaret was very, very good with her neighbours. If a person felt ill she went out to get things for them: beef for a broth or a nice sponge. She cleaned the house thoroughly for them."

If she found that an elderly person didn't have much coal in the cellar, she would make arrangements for a sack of coal to be delivered. In such cases and when shopping for the sick or elderly she usually paid for the items out of her own money.

When asked by Helen if the people had given her the money Margaret said that she did not look for payment or any recompense. When a doctor was due to call on an elderly person Margaret would help them to get ready for the visit.

She carried out her charitable work quietly and without fuss or show. While ready to help others she was in no way intrusive. She didn't talk about her kindly visits. Helen would ask: "Where is Margaret this evening?" and be told that she had gone to visit someone who was ill.

Margaret cheerfully put up with personal inconvenience to help others. During one lunch time she met a religious sister who was carrying a heavy bag, near the church of St Cuthbert's where Margaret often spent time in prayer before the Blessed Sacrament. She offered to carry the bag but the sister refused and they compromised by both carrying it.

In conversation Margaret mentioned her work as a French-polisher and said she would be happy to do any work of that nature at the convent. The sister told her that there was a desk in need of treatment and Margaret agreed to go along after work. However, when Margaret arrived at the convent, in the evening, having travelled a considerable distance to get there, she learnt that the Superior thought it was too late for her to begin work on the desk. Margaret was not in the least put out by this but happily went into the garden with the sister she had originally spoken to and they talked about convent life in general. She was unperturbed by her wasted journey.

When Margaret's mother volunteered her to help a neighbour with her correspondence Margaret felt considerable embarrassment but complied with her usual willingness. To make matters worse, Margaret found that the person concerned used lengthy words which she didn't know how to spell. She felt ashamed that despite her education she was still ignorant of these things.

She was much more at ease when it came to using a needle. She used to go with Bella to the Convent of the Helpers of the Holy Souls, in Drummond Place, near her home, to take part in the task of mending vestments and altar linen from the cathedral. Margaret was happy to do the more difficult work and was willing to learn. During these sewing sessions they used to hear about the missionary work being carried out by the Order. It was something that Margaret always enjoyed.

If she heard an appeal for clothes for the poor or for missionary work, she would respond by buying some material and making clothes. When she and Bella were out together, and saw poor children in torn clothes, Margaret used to say how she wished they had enough money to get clothes for all of them.

She liked to make donations to the Society of St Vincent de Paul for its work among the poor and she encouraged others to put something into the Society's box for offerings in the church. Despite her limited resources a good many people in the area received alms from Margaret. An old man without legs, who used to sit outside St Patrick's Church, regularly received money from Margaret who went down to see him. Other elderly people received money from her to help them get some shopping. Contributions to the Association for the Propagation of the Faith reflected her great interest in the foreign missions.

Sometimes the money she gave to others was not just for essentials but for little "extras" such as sweets for the children.

Love for her neighbour was in no way confined to the material. Margaret showed concern and compassion regarding the spiritual welfare of others, giving thought, time and prayer.

There were quite a number of Catholics living in Blackfriars Street but many were non-practising. Margaret gently tried to persuade neighbours who had lapsed to return to the Mass and the Sacraments. She encouraged people to attend Missions and similar events in the parish. Household chores and several children contributed to the reason why one neighbour no longer went to Mass. So, Margaret helped out in the woman's home in order to give her time to take up the practice of her religion once again.

Regarding lapsed Catholics Margaret used to say: "Perhaps they would not have lost the faith if they had been properly instructed." She gave pamphlets to such people, prayed for them and did penance for them. She would say that perhaps they had not had the opportunities that she and her family had had. Margaret was quick to make excuses for the failings of others, saying that the person had not really meant it or that it was in their nature and they could not act differently. She used to say to a friend: "Well, we don't know their situation. All we can do is say a wee prayer for them."

Her compassion for sinners could be seen in her words: "Poor souls, if only they knew how Our Lord is ready to help them..." There was a good deal of drunkenness and swearing in Blackfriars Street, particularly at weekends.

The celebration of the New Year also gave rise to much drunkenness, bottle-throwing and shouting in the street.

Margaret always asked people to pray for those who got drunk, rather than condemn them. She hated to hear the name of God or Jesus taken in vain but, again, her reaction was to offer praise to God in reparation, to pray for those concerned and ask others to pray as well.

Her concern for sinners went further than just praying for them. Her sister-in-law, Helen, noticed on one occasion that Margaret jumped and an expression of pain fleetingly appeared on her face when she gave her a friendly pat on the back. Helen was alarmed: "Oh, Margaret, did I hurt you?" "No," said Margaret. "Then why did you jump just now?" Margaret said she wore a small cross on her back. When asked why, Margaret replied: "To save some souls." She said no more; and when Helen mentioned it to her husband, John, he said he knew about it but that Margaret didn't like to discuss it. The cross in question was, in fact, a small wooden one into which Margaret had inserted several small nails or tacks, with pointed ends protruding. This was a painful penance in the ordinary way but, when friends patted her on the back, the nails dug into her.

Lizzie could not recall Margaret ever having said an inconsiderate word to anyone. A friend stated: "I never heard her say a harsh word about anyone." If she had nothing good to say about a person she would not say anything.

Margaret's love for her neighbour extended beyond this life to those who had died but were still in need of prayer. She had a great love for the Holy Souls and contributed to having Mass offered for them. She often spoke about them and encouraged people to remember them in their prayers.

The charitable work that Margaret undertook for others had, of course, to be done in her spare time. As her working day lasted from 8 a.m. to 6 p.m., and often included a lengthy journey to and from work, there was not a great deal of spare time but she cheerfully gave that time.

The brief holidays that Margaret had with Bella were in no way holidays from helping others. At Rosewell, the cottage they stayed in was far from luxurious. Water had to be drawn from a well some fifty yards away. The village store was a mile away. The two sisters were noted for their cheerfulness and their willingness to help the elderly couple who lived in the cottage — shopping and washing-up for them, not to mention some housework. When the girls' mother came to visit them the elderly woman in the cottage exclaimed how happy Mrs Sinclair must be to have two children like them.

In her relationships with her neighbours, near and far, it is possible to see Margaret as the cheerful giver, whether it was a matter of generosity in time — willingly giving the spare time she had after a full-day's work and her share of the household tasks in her family — generosity in giving to the poor from the limited amount she had or generosity in her attempts to find excuses for other people and to make reparation for their faults and failings.

Margaret's love of neighbour was not something that simply took place in her spare time. The manner in which she carried out her work also shows her as the cheerful giver.

She did her best with anything she took on and this included her work as a French-polisher. One person who saw her at work was impressed by the care with which she worked and the beautiful results of her skills. She used to say: "You need patience for this type of work." Her employers were well-satisfied with her conscientious approach and the results of her painstaking efforts.

She not only prayed at work but saw work itself as a form of prayer which she could offer to God.

Margaret was a willing witness to the faith, in her various work-places. She wore on her overalls the badge of the Handmaids of the Blessed Sacrament. Another Catholic girl asked her if she wasn't afraid to wear it at work, where most people were Protestants. (These were in generally pre-ecumenical times and anti-Catholicism was far from rare.) Margaret replied: "I would like the whole world to know I am a Catholic!" By wearing the badge and openly acknowledging her Catholicism she hoped to encourage a similar, fearless acknowledgement among other Catholic workers.

In one place she found a picture of the Blessed Virgin in a pile of rubbish. She dusted it and put it up near where she worked. The following day she came in and found that it had been taken down. She put it up again; the next morning it had been removed. Not to be outdone, she replaced it once more. The following day it was still in its place but with the face turned to the wall. And so the silent battle continued.

She actually spoke very little about her faith, in the work-place. Her witness was given quietly and effectively through her manner and the way she worked. If any worker tried to tell her coarse jokes she firmly and silently ignored them. They soon got the message and left her in peace. In the cloak-room of one firm Margaret found that her hat had been thrown on the floor. She made no complaint but said to Bella: "These little things can be put up with for the love of God."

As Margaret grew up it was the love of God and of his will which became central to her whole life. It gave rise to her untiring love of neighbour. It led to a total giving of herself to God in the religious life and a whole-hearted acceptance of the illness that developed almost immediately after her religious profession.

5

Everything to God

"I want to be all his." That was what Margaret told Fr Agius when she went to speak to him about her wish to follow the religious life, with the Poor Clares. Fr Agius had pointed out to her that marriage was a great sacrament, and the life of the Poor Clares was very hard. Was she sure that she didn't want to get married, he asked her.

Margaret was certain. The inner conviction that she was being called to give her life to Christ in the religious life had been growing stronger and stronger. She wanted to be "all his". She had been a cheerful giver in her family and among her friends and neighbours for the sake of Christ; now she wanted to make the total gift of herself to him. She loved her family greatly, and had a warm affection for her friends, but she was willing to go away from them in order to come closer to Christ in a life of prayer and penance. She was particularly drawn by the poverty of the Poor Clares. The more she could give up for God, the happier she seemed to be.

Margaret's giving to God was something

that grew as she grew from childhood to adulthood. It involved vigilance on her part in order to cooperate with the grace of God in overcoming her natural tendencies and faults, such as her impatience. Bella said that virtue did not come naturally to Margaret and that Margaret had said she needed to exercise a great deal of self-control.

When Margaret was still a child each Advent and Lent found her busy reciting prayers and counting them by marking a cross for each prayer on a piece of card. The crosses numbered hundreds. The prayers were her gift to the Lord at Christmas and Easter. As she grew up she no longer marked the prayers on a card but she became increasingly prayerful.

While at school Margaret took part in the customary monthly Communion, but after leaving school and starting work she went to daily Mass and Communion. It was the most important part of each day for her, and love for the Eucharist formed a framework for her day.

On weekdays she liked to extend her devotion to the Eucharist by going into a church at lunch time and spending time in adoration. She would again call into a church for a few moments after work. On Sundays, there was no rushing to work after Mass, and so Margaret would return home for breakfast and then go to her room to continue her thanksgiving before helping with the preparations for lunch.

Her attitude towards daily Communion was that people should go in order that the Lord could make them holy, not because they were already holy. Margaret had little confidence in herself, said her mother, but trusted in God for everything. She used to say: "We are poor souls without God."

Margaret enjoyed going to parish dances and socials with members of her family but when she returned home she would always insist on saying the rosary before going to bed, even if it was after midnight. She said that they had enjoyed themselves, now they must give God his share. Lizzie remembered that Margaret, leading the rosary, would sometimes forget the number of "Hail Mary's" she had recited and continue past the ten in a decade to twelve or more whereupon Lizzie would exclaim that they were never going to get to bed at that rate.

As a child Margaret had willingly given up things for Lent such as sugar in her tea or anything on her bread. Her spirit of penance developed as she got older. One night, after Margaret and her sisters had gone to bed, their mother started to go quietly into the room to get something from a drawer but, while Bella and Lizzie were asleep, Margaret was kneeling on the floor with her arms outstretched in prayer. She did not hear her mother who tiptoed out and closed the door. Margaret's nocturnal prayer sessions were also a penance because she needed a considerable amount of sleep. Sometimes, in the evening, she would nod off in the chair. But, with her prayer in the night, she was practising for the austere life to which she had begun to feel drawn.

Margaret was always enthusiastic about her faith. When it came to sermons she did not mind who was preaching — she found food for thought regardless of whether it was considered a "good" or "bad" sermon. She looked for opportunities to learn more about her faith. Lizzie said that Margaret always thanked God for the gift of faith. She was more than happy that people should know she was a Catholic even when it drew some unpleasant remarks at work.

Her response to the vocation to become a religious was whole-hearted. She willingly made the sacrifice of leaving her well-loved family and her homeland. We know that she had her "ups and downs" in the convent but she remained cheerful. Her generous spirit can be seen not only in her choice of one of the more austere Orders but also in her decision to enter as an extern sister which was considered a far more lowly position that than of the enclosed choir nuns. The extern sisters looked after the needs of the enclosed nuns; they maintained some contact with the outside world while the choir nuns remained in their enclosure. The rare occasions when the extern sisters were allowed into the enclosure were seen as being a great privilege for them. Margaret was happy with her lowly position.

Her attitude towards her life as a Poor Clare can be seen in the resolutions she made during a retreat: "I will be submissive in all things, always having before me that my Lord, my God, was ever submissive to St Joseph and obedient even unto the death of the cross. I will practise charity in my words and ever look out for little opportunities to perfect this beautiful virtue in helping my Sisters, especially in those things that are contrary to my nature. I will endeavour to be diligent, always to try and do all things well, and ever to have a pure intention in what I do. This year, please God, I desire to vow to you my poverty, chastity and obedience, and, to observe the same, to rejoice when I feel the pinch of poverty. And always to remain modest and prudent, thinking of this in our Blessed Lady and how she would like it in her child."

Did she have her "ups and downs" in mind when she composed a prayer for the First Station of the Cross, where Jesus is condemned to death?

"O my Jesus, help me to think of this often and give me the grace to accept all unjust criticism in the same way as I desire to do in all things your holy will."

The spirit of the cheerful giver can be seen in the prayer she composed for the Second Station of the Cross, where Jesus receives his crosss.

"O my Jesus, you accept it with patience and resignation, as you desired our Redemption. You think not of the suffering it will cost you or your Immaculate Mother, but only of saving us poor miserable sinners from the abyss of hell. O my God, help me always to take up your cross cheerfully and follow you."

The greatest test for Margaret's cheerfulness and spirit of generosity came with her illness, diagnosed almost immediately after her profession in the Poor Clares. Throughout her life she had often referred to the will of God, regarding all that happened as being his will. She did the same when this blow fell.

She was under no illusions about her illness. Soon after she became ill she wrote to Bella saying that she thought she would soon be with their father. She did not pray for a cure but was completely resigned to whatever God wanted of her. When her mother expressed the hope that the Lord would soon take her out of her sufferings Margaret gently chided her: "You mustn't speak like that, Mother, because God will not take me before my time."

When Margaret went through a particularly bad period of suffering she would whisper: "My Jesus, mercy. Your will be done." She showed no impatience. The Superior at Warley said: "She accepted all the sufferings of her last illness with complete joy, for the love of God." The same sister stated that Margaret "wanted nothing but the will of God". She had not found the slightest imperfection in Margaret, she said.

Margaret surrendered herself completely to God and offered her sufferings for the salvation of souls but she continued also to give help and encouragement to those around her and to spread cheerfulness.

When one of the sisters at Warley discovered that Margaret came from Scotland, like herself, they used to joke and tease each other about their respective cities of Edinburgh and Glasgow.

On one occasion Margaret noticed that one of the sisters had been in tears following a reprimand from another sister. She whispered words of encouragement to her, speaking of carrying a little piece of the cross. The sister described Margaret as very kind. "She tried to make everyone smile." It was the same Margaret who, years before, had been trying to make other children happy by giving them "swings". She was still trying to cheer people up, despite her own increasing sufferings.

When her family came to visit her, her brother, John, laughed so loudly at the stories she was relating that Margaret had to tell him to laugh more quietly so that he didn't disturb the other patients. Even when she became too ill to speak much she would give a smile to the sister who looked after her if she heard her come into the room.

The sisters at Warley never could find out Margaret's preferences in food. One of them said: "She took everything with a sweet smile. When something was taken to her she used to say: 'How good the Lord is to me: he spoils me.'" On one occasion it was forgotten to give her her dinner. When the sister finally arrived with the meal, apologizing for being so late and for the food being spoiled, Margaret made no complaint but simply smiled and assured her that what had been brought to her was just what she liked.

Those who looked after her commented on how grateful she always was for anything that was done for her. She was particularly grateful for the visits made to her by sisters from her own convent, and asked them on their last visit to tell the Mother Abbess that she was truly grateful for everything that had been done for her and wished to thank everyone. When one of the sisters at Warley asked Margaret to remember her in heaven she replied: "Yes, Sister, I shall never forget you."

When her mother, John and Lizzie came to see her for the last time, about a month before she died, her main concern was to impress upon Lizzie the need to look after her mother. "Remember, Lizzie, to do all you can to make Mother's life a little easier, and never leave her alone." Margaret knew how bereft her mother must be feeling now that most of the children had left home and their father had died.

Before the family left the sanatorium Margaret reassured her mother: "Now, Mother, go home and don't be afraid. I am in the hands of God." She said she would pray for them in heaven. "Goodbye, I will see you again in heaven," were her parting words to her mother.

Margaret had always had a special devotion to the name of Jesus and had the name written on a card which she kept near her bed. She loved to place flowers around the card. When she made the final gift of herself to God, through death, it was the name of Jesus that was on her lips.

§

6

Margaret: an example for today

The Second Vatican Council stressed the universal call to holiness and underlined the fact that each person would arrive at the holiness to which they were called by God, at Baptism, in and through the circumstances of their daily lives and work. This makes Margaret Sinclair a particularly appropriate example for Christians today. It was the very simplicity of her life that makes her so.

We may not be called to found religious orders or to work in distant mission fields. We may not be given the opportunity for martyrdom. We may be — most likely will be — just ordinary people leading common-or-garden lives with a share of joys and sorrows, such as come to all human beings. But the call to holiness is there and, as the Council impressed upon us, is one to be taken seriously by all.

For twenty-three of her twenty-five years, Margaret lived as a lay person, leading a normal family life, and for nine of those years she went out to work. The ways in which she helped her family and her neighbour were the sorts of ways in which most people would be able to help others.

When she joined the Poor Clares, there was nothing outwardly unusual in her life as a postulant and as a novice. She simply, faithfully, carried out her duties. When she became ill, the illness followed its normal course and Margaret grew further in holiness by cheerfully accepting the situation.

Vatican II spoke of how the people could grow in holiness through the conditions, duties and circumstances of their lives: "These things will be the means of their advance in holiness, if they combine their faith with an acceptance of everything which comes from the hand of their heavenly Father and if they are cooperative with the divine will, making in the very service of this life, a demonstration to all men of the charity with which God has loved the world" (*Lumen Gentium*, 41).

As Margaret grew up it was clear to those around her that the will of God was the centre of her life and that she accepted everything as being God's will. This, in turn, led her to believe firmly that all would be well in the end. She trusted God as her heavenly Father and encouraged others to do the same. In the gentle kindness she showed to others, in ordinary ways, Margaret reflected the loving-kindness of God. Even more did she reflect that love in her concern for sinners — praying for them, finding excuses for their behaviour, doing penance for them, accepting her sufferings for them, and asking other people to pray for them.

"The true disciple of Christ carries the mark of charity towards God and his neighbour," said the Council (*Lumen Gentium*, 42). Pointing to the vital need for charity to grow and bear fruit within each person, the Council reiterated: "Each individual believer then must give the word of God a willing hearing, do God's will, take part in the sacraments, especially the Eucharist, and sacred actions, apply himself steadily to prayer, self-denial, active brotherly charity, the practice of all the virtues with the help of his grace" (*Lumen Gentium*, 42).

Margaret was someone who did all those things, simply, quietly, without fuss, in her daily life. At an age when, today, many young people stop going to Mass, she began the practice of daily Mass and Communion. Her life was permeated with prayer, as she went about her work and took part in various leisure activities with her family.

Self-control, putting others first, and moderation in food and drink, were among the ways in which she practised self-denial. She gave a willing hearing to the word of God, through reading and thinking about the Scriptures, and through eagerly drawing spiritual nourishment from sermons and missions.

Without the example of people like Margaret Sinclair we might be tempted to think that the Council was indulging in some wishful thinking when it said: "All Christ's faithful have an invitation, which is binding, to the pursuit of holiness and perfection in their own station of life" (*Lumen Gentium*, 42).

The call to holiness and perfection is not exactly a new one! There are Christ's words: "You, therefore, must be perfect, as your heavenly Father is perfect" (Mt 5:48). But, somehow, we have tended to think that even if those words were indeed meant for everyone rather than a few heroic souls, then only a small minority would actually succeed in becoming truly holy in this life.

Margaret shows the feasibility of countless Christians cooperating with the grace of God to become holy. Looking at Margaret's life we should be led to look at our own lives and see where there are more ways in which we, too, can give cheerfully to God and to those around us.

Margaret teaches us another important lesson, namely, how we should view holiness. Having the wrong idea about it means we would miss it even if it were right under our noses. There were those who knew St Therese of Lisieux but laughed at the idea of canonizing her. There was a similar reaction from some who knew Margaret.

The extraordinary happenings that occur in the lives of some holy people make fascinating reading. In the past, lives of saints were often written as though one marvellous event succeeded another. This only helped to put holiness, or the wrong ideas about it, further and further away from the lives of ordinary people. Saints seemed to be born rather than made or, if they had been converted from a life of sin, it appeared that they henceforth led perfect lives. These ideas seemed a long way from the real experience of Christians everywhere.

A friend of Margaret Sinclair, who admired her greatly, said that she had been no plaster saint. There are, of course, no plaster saints — only flesh-and-blood human ones. They grow to love God with all their hearts, minds and souls, and their neighbours as themselves, only because they are open to the Holy Spirit and cooperate with God's abundant grace.

Each person is unique, and his or her relationship with God will be unique. Therefore, each of us has to listen, to try to find out what path the Lord calls us to follow in order that we may become truly and fully ourselves — with and in the Risen Lord. For most of us it will be a path which, in its simplicity, its ordinariness, will be very similar to the one walked by Margaret Sinclair. If, like her, we make full and generous use of the talents given to us we shall also, like her, reap an abundant harvest of holiness.

Thoughts from Margaret

"You don't necessarily have to be always on your knees when you pray."

"Pray with perseverance; if you do not obtain what you ask for the first time, persevere."

"Don't worry about anything. Just put your trust in God and everything will be all right in time."

"Put your worries into the hands of God and everything will be all right."

"God never asks difficult things without giving the help for them."

"We cannot go through life without having something of the cross."

"We would be poor souls without God."

"Without God we cannot do anything; with his help we can do much."

"To bring the sun into the lives of others, it is necessary to keep it always alight in ourselves."

"There are no bad days."

"If Catholics gave good example, it would bring lapsed Catholics back to the faith."

Selected Bibliography

Burton D.E., *Margaret Sinclair*, the Margaret Sinclair Centre.

Forbes F.A., *Margaret Sinclair*, Sands, London, (4th ed.) 1930.

Johnston F.E., *Margaret Sinclair*, Catholic Truth Society, London.

Sacred Congregation for the Causes of Saints: *Positio super virtutibus* (relating to the Cause of Margatet Sinclair), Rome, 1965. *Relatio et vota peculiaris Congressus*; and *Responsio Patroni ad difficultates in relatione adnotatas* (relating to the Cause of Margaret Sinclair), Rome 1976.

Venerable Margaret Sinclair – The Warley Story, published by the Association of Friends of Margaret Sinclair, Warley, 1980.

NO GREATER LOVE
Damien apostle of the lepers

by John Milsome

This is the story of a man – Joseph de Veuster, better known as Father Damien, "the hero of Molokai" – who devoted his life to the welfare of the lepers on the island of Molokai, in the Pacific Ocean. The conditions on the island were daunting. The lepers lived in squalor and misery. Being a foreigner he was not at once welcomed by the lepers. His "ragged honesty, generosity and mirth" however, won them over as friends.

What is Damien's relevance for us today? Basically three things: fidelity to one's calling, dedication to a worthy cause and compassion for the underprivileged and outcasts of society.

Robert Louis Stevenson wrote of Damien: "It was his part, by one striking act of martyrdom, to direct all men's eyes on this distressful country. At a blow and with the price of his life, he made the place illustrious and public... If ever any man brought reforms and died to bring them, it was he." This is the challenge unfolded in the pages of *No Greater Love*.

JOHN MILSOME was born in Pinner, Middlesex. He trained as a teacher and his main interest outside teaching was his writing career. The completion of No Greater Love *was sealed with his premature death*.

THROUGH THE EYE OF A NEEDLE
Frederick Ozanam

by Austin Fagan

A 20-year old student, Frederick Ozanam, and some of his friends, founded the Society of St Vincent de Paul in 1833. This was a time when the Church in France was the object of bitter hostility, following the revolutions of 1789 and 1830. Rather than involve themselves in political controversy and seek ways of reforming the world, the founding-members of the SVP looked for a more immediate and practical way in which to alleviate some of the poverty and suffering of those less fortunate in life.

The first part of the book is a dramatized account of Frederick Ozana's life, while the second part presents reflections on some of his ideas expressed in his writings and in many of his university lectures and other talks. His influence led many others to follow him by seeking Christ in the poor whether they are spiritually, physically or materially deprived.

A book which reveals how Frederick's was a truly prophetic voice that still inspires many in the Church to speak out and act on behalf of the poor and the underprivileged of society.

THE HAPPINESS OF GOD
Holiness in Therese of Lisieux

by Susan Leslie

According to the best masters of spirituality a solid foundation of holiness is to give oneself to God in such a way that *his good pleasure* becomes one's joy. Therese of Lisieux had this magnificent obsession: *to see God happy*.

As she lay dying in September 1897, at the age of 24, she claimed that all her actions had been performed with that single aim. *Making God happy* was Therese programme of life and holiness. This is the target she sets, even today, before the multitude of "little souls" whom she hopes to carry along her "little way" to heaven.

SUSAN LESLIE is a contemplative nun and lives in Oxford.

IMAGES OF HOLINESS

Series Editor: Felicity O'Brien, B.A.
Consultant Editor: Fr Paul Molinari, S.J.,
Professor of Spiritual Theology at the Gregorian
University, Rome; Chairman of the College of
Postulators.*

1. THE CHEERFUL GIVER
   Margaret Sinclair by Felicity O'Brien

2. NO GREATER LOVE
   Damien apostle of the lepers by John Milsome

In preparation:

3. THROUGH THE EYE OF A NEEDLE
   Frederick Ozanam by Austin Fagan

Postulators promote the causes of candidates for beatification or canonization.